The Tales In Thoughts Of Restless Spirit

Frank Schroeder

FRANK SCHROEDER

ISBN 978-1-64515-977-3 (paperback)
ISBN 978-1-64515-978-0 (digital)

Christian Faith Publishing, Inc.
832 Park Avenue
Meadville, PA 16335
www.christianfaithpublishing.com

Printed in the United States of America

Preface

Praise be to our Lord, of a soul, who has lost one's way with Christ. To search the world for his life, where learned in scripture:

what is worldly lost of one's life,
for Christ's sake,
is life everlasting to be gained.

Gone yesterday is what we leave behind today. By what starts out as darkness, eventually wind up in the light of God's love; when our love sees past ourselves, within his word. And faith gives us hope, for our love to see past what the world wants, to put others before us. It is what we do to each other that defines who we are. For by their fruits, you shall know them. To be with God is an open heart, in an empty cup, being filled with life through Jesus Christ.

Mankind has been farsighted on dreams pursued but short-sighted being among ourselves. The world we look at, is what looks back, from a conscience within heart of mind by its soul. Where fault lies not so much in the free will of choice, as does, within ourselves. It is the choice we make in every day decisions, of that hope in rationality prevailing, for discerning wisely. In the end are the consequences we are held accountable for, upon a conscience, that should be. Without God (the father), Jesus Christ (the son), and Holy Spirit (spirit of God, the comforter); words like love, faith, and hope, would have as much meaning as wishing on a star, by what is true. We need to learn how to stand up for the truth, when we know it.

If a picture can tell a thousand words, then a thousand words should portray a picture. This book depicts the collective thoughts, in poems, of an individual who fell away from God. Then embarks on a dark, arduous journey back home to find his life. Only to eventually find it, through faith in Jesus Christ.

For those of you who believe, I hope you never stray from a home, of a father, whose love was never lost for you. As I have done.

And for those who are searching for your life. I hope you find it in Jesus Christ; as I did.

To let the relevance in life possibly reflect what is written in these poems. To keep the aspect of an open mind and heart, to prevail in understanding by where insight of your being stands in you. Not from values dictated by man, but the moral virtues as a principle held, to grow into of our own free will, given by God. For the hope to change in time, that someday, we maybe become accountable for.

A Fall from Grace

Evil that besiege upon men's hearts,
restless goes into the night;
to the darkness, begins its ominous creep,
fallen be of twilight;
Now home, be the soul it seems,
becomes a foreign sight;
so far away, the distance be,
returning is dimmed by time;
That fall from grace, from there so high
across light-years, amongst the bitter plight,
deceived by sin, the hypocrisy of pride;
The truth within, seek and we may find,
where pain felt in sorrowful hurt,
to alert, with all ears and eyes;
There before many dreams seen, have heard,
the words to bring light;
that seeks by Lord's way,
make life again right;…

To loneliness, belongs the soul of their own fears,
calling out for help,
drowning in a sea of people, alone;
only to fall upon deaf ears,
where everyone for themselves,
there, to each their own.

We are all sinners in ourselves alone,
but together, we are saved,
when in Jesus Christ known,

Francis Schroeder

Standing on the Precipice

Facing the turbulent winds of fate,
on precarious grounds,
eerie befalls approaching storms before thee, to await;
while darkly crisis has amassed,
bringing adversity abound.

Standing on razor's edge,
try not to stand too tall,
beware of anger's bitter pledge,
may become the pride before the fall;

Turmoil is a labyrinth in its confusion,
of walking among land mines,
on experience of defining moments to decide,
when life can become a walk into suicide;

It is by the decision
that you decide,
that will forever echo
with you throughout time;

A remnant of truth, gone by,
deception becomes subjective, to mind,
images seen through windows of the eyes
from reality to surreal, reflects the thoughts described,

Expect that of what is unexpected,
as to be warned to anticipate;
foreboding into darkness, the ominous be undetected,
to what trepidation will face that be,
to fight the unseen,
the evil that comes this way,

The enemy all around,
where they have always been,
from delusion of security therein,
to reflections of a mirror akin,
now see the enemy from within;

How far will knowledge go without virtue,
a life debased can be sold or bought,
take caution; the snares for traps conceived
by illusions,
where there are many often caught

–impassioned, the life by lies,
is the heart of a fool's demise–

Apathy born of complacency at home,
where opportunity awaits in freedom known;
then there before your very life,
thus are the jackals of tyranny, incognito,
to devour all your rights;
now home is what you look for in refuge
running from your plight;

For what is beneath you,
taken for granted in mind,
may soon be nothing to stand on,
where foundation lies;

Strange is the experience,
as a teacher of the sort,
first you are tested, hence,
then you are taught;

And if salvation be of our sanity prevails,
to keep in trim;
from destruction's aftermath survived by what ails;
to be saved from the retribution for our sins;
keeping your head about you, is the victory within;
being alive that makes you stronger therein;
is all of its joy, that has always been

Francis Schroeder

In a Conscience of Belief

How much time spent
in values sowed,
where righteousness
has no free will to roam;

A price, there to be owed,
when something given
is by sheep who lie that know;
"by way of what is evil cloaked"

What is mind without a conscience,
becomes just as much,
flesh without a soul;

What pain here is in heart,
begotten in slavery of where sin goes,
when that sorrow
that is part of you,
calls out from the cold,

For a person
by oneself,
is a person alone;
but a soul
among a blind crowd,
is a soul lost,
that cannot find in God
a home;

Where,
from here,
do we go,
what we will become,
from what we follow—
in a world that is to deny the truth,
or accept it so,
within a life composed.

Francis Schroeder

Our Time in Life

Moral are the elite,
only by their own predication,
the hypocrisy of words said from emotions sworn;
born is virtuous,
when true as the garden grows—
from the parents, love is in its name;… The Lord known;

If the unjust, where arrogance be its own deceit,
were to open their eyes,
to the truth of a fate unseen,
it would remain ongoing undenied,
that life exist for God being;

Time stops for no grain of sand fallen,
where there is no escape to defend,
held prisoner by their own convictions,
answering accountable then;
unrepented at a place in time by them all,
stand before abandoned cries forsaken,
are the echoed lives that call;

Conception is life beginning,
for time to forego,
to conceive, is God's blessing,
to walk down dawn's narrow road,
for most who there go,
we are born of a thought in time unknown;

We take a leap in faith,
on a journey to our fate,
for a destiny to be sown;

Only to bring us back again,
in convictions of a belief beholden
to our origins,
in a place we finally have come to known;

Francis Schroeder

On Razor's Edge

Part I

False witness spurs in arrogance to despise so insidiously,
that treachery come this way,
the collusion to incite self-righteousness with hypocrisy,
selfish the pride, that are inroads to betray;

Distortion be progressive upon truth, encroaching paths to stray;
from their master's den, they learned to play;
the control that alludes to, once upon a masquerade,
all the world becomes their stage,
owned by the words of a persona portrayed,
known by their follower's rage,
where danger lurks,
in death that flirts;
within the deadly charades;

From the sum of all inequity's illusions,
found in education taught to our young,
may reflect of our enemies past oppressive solutions,
that could be in the end,
without God in heart
the future we become;

Francis Schroeder

From the Razor's Edge

Part 2

Tyrants long for to usurp power and control,
anarchist are the coercion
that compel the silence of lambs atoned,
the cowardice to be found in the fear known,
a means to an end,
to that, seems condoned;

When the righteous
are constrained to be silenced in all,
then foundations of a free society
will cause to erode,
where pride alone standing before
onto a nation,
into itself
will fall;

On road to retribution,
truth be the fire of soul,
that burns judgment cold,
of convictions within;

things in life do change,
let not reason be thrown,
leave be well enough alone,
to let understanding remain;

What one does not see,
is seen by another,
together in Christ,
peace be alive in love, as sisters and brothers;

A purpose for existence being,
a reason for all things,
a season in time for doing, deemed;
the world as a family, in God's glory;

Francis Schroeder

Epilogue

Part 3

In games of hawks and doves,
that people play,
manifest of the world, it seems persuaded,
to that be in the things they love;

Grace be the mercy, found in wounded souls
out of sadness comes into joy,
presence be in the Lord,
great in thine known,
to let healing be shown;

Dauntless the search, on beaten paths to go;
harmony are but notes
of a song in heart,
sung in the nature of its essence,
from afar,
to a life God has created
is of what you make it,
where purpose exist to fit.

Francis Schroeder

The Injustice

Condescending reflects of divisiveness, the tribunal thoughts;
trial by emotions, a state of mind to that sort;
the social regressions, are in restless spirits lost;

Accused becomes the accusers,
when distorted the truth, be of accusations incurred,
stand represented by irrational users;

Petty the results, are falsehoods in shallowness,
come true to heart the cowardice,
that is faceless;

So what becomes
of the soul in conscience
within a soul of body,
that becomes us,

In a world of where lives are torn,
there "is" none righteous anymore,
when all are in the wrong.

Francis Schroeder

After the Fall

In the things you seek,
you may never find;
the things you find,
you may never keep;
and there are more than a thousand ways in life
to run down time,
to certain defeat;

Humility is the reality,
that puts life in its place—
in all that is love, for not to contend;
the means by which, is justified in the end,

There is no pride,
no vanity,
nor does it boast in face,
you cannot walk away and just pretend,

In meekness, we humble the heart in mind of thought,
to be one with Christ, is living his cause;

Burdensome within, be this pain,
a new character in me, to be gained,
in Christ, we are saved by grace,
the works in faith, we place;

Then freedom be the eternal
in its righteousness that has always been;
when infinite to a life,
is reborn again,
in a conscience anew to begin;

Wiped away will be our tears,
in end of days;
the future we see, no longer feared,
in the Lord we pray

To know oneself be true,
from darkness of sinful man,
worthy is the Lamb,
for true to faith be in us,
that we take our stand.

Francis Schroeder

Of Restless Spirits

Of spiritual war, in the aftermath befalls
who won?
in a thousand yards of stare can tell,
with Christ it is done;

What does profit one in soul,
without so much the premise,
of asking the Lord
for wisdom to know;

Lost and lonely be in dismay,
for to the darkness, does not remain,
where light of morning looms to reign,
things are always possible with God,
in his own way;

The lion will always know its place,
in the wilderness;
the wind never stays long,
in time of test,

If hope
is to come from faith,
then stronger should we stand before crisis,
that we may face;

Where love finding endless,
is for life's purpose of given grace,
there bringing home to find rest,
for a restless spirit to elate;

And by what we inherit to heir
in the peace to be found,
we will find it there,
forevermore, to be around.

Francis Schroeder

In Worlds Apart

In worlds apart, seems concern that problems be,
far from a time away we once knew;
just to see beyond a dream,
that takes up with faith in thee,
the meaning for life to hold true;

Can ever in conscience deep,
a righteous generation be in lifetime taught;
or will there always be battlefields to cross;

Turmoil is the season of storms.
rough be the road traveled
on mountain path;
love brings the summer's warmth,
from light of spring
out of darkness past;

Bought is not happiness, ensued
but made with wise choices, to pursue;

Christ gives us the truth,
for the way,
of the life,
at its best;

In the year of living prayer by our progress,
while on this earth before we die,
is that trust in God we live by,
prepares the yield for time of harvest;

Planted are the seeds,
in every word he said,
that exhales of life,
with his every breath;

For there are none greater than he,
whose spirit that lives in you,
than in all the world to live for,
to being abreast

Francis Schroeder

Unforsaken

Standing upon time,
where life is too cold to keep,
let not this heart be harden,
in a world of inhumanity,

Faith
That lives by bread alone,
is a life mundane,
that lives in mediocrity;

Blind are the wise
who pretend to believe,
just as those who have eyes with sight,
but refuse to see;

Quenched be this thirst,
from springs of waters deep,
for faith to die not,
in the sins of humanity's sea;

Faith,
can move mountains aside;
can bring the azure to cloudy skies;
can calm the stormy seas
can make a victory
out of an inevitable defeat;

Faith is patience that be a virtue
by birth from wisdom;
giving substance to hope for you,
believing in thing's unseen to come;

From beginning to the end,
life may grow out of planted seeds,
learned is the message to comprehend.
faith delivers truth by trust in its belief;

Never fear, to be forgotten by his love,
while you look toward the heavens for signs;
for where Christ is there in you by faith,
with the Lord, you are never left behind.

Francis Schroeder

Waiting in the Wing

Expanding,
only to contract,
much impatience to erupt
are abound;

Are we to become
as animals,
at the behest
of when jealousy sounds;

From the fires
that burns within you
all your illusions
come tumbling down;

Whoever finds their life,
will lose it,
whoever loses their life
for thine sake
will be as one who is found;

Light of the son,
upon solar winds;
words of light,
true of conviction;
food for the soul
that stands renowned;

The feeling to live,
can start out from almost nothing,
and leave behind a legacy
to be crowned

Francis Schroeder

A Time for Letting Go

Darkness follows shadows,
when sorrows suffers broken hearts
in wounded souls;

When the rapacious
relentlessly gives no repose,
how far can one endure forever to go;
how much do answers to questions really know;
how deep truly is a soul,
for where the pain to go;

By what today brings in sorrows,
may be what is demanded
for justice tomorrow;
love least be forgiveness for God's glory,
that compassion be of our morals;

Time measures the harvest that grows,
from what seeds of one's conscience
will sow;

To cross that bridge
toward where narrow path goes;
never looking back to dwell
on what was known;
leaving behind
the confessions of sins to forgo,
to thine be told;

Better for departing with sorrows
are into letting go,
when unconditionally,
God's love perseveres the healing of souls
to give character, foretold,
that of within
"hope"

Francis Schroeder

A Time to Cast Away Stones

Echoes that sound the night,
lonely is a soul in its plight,
hard is the life in its time,
when answers are the question left to be,
left behind;

Life can elude
the walk in faith,
where concerns the status
are of worldly sights, left to our fate;

Chosen may the path be,
of a life for permanency,
or a world so temporary;
with everybody, lies their own destiny,
upon them, it may weigh heavily;

Never a beggar be to sin
in this life,
where time is borrowed;
character is born of hope from perseverance,
out of sufferings,
strengthen by righteous sorrows;

In the light of truth
Known,
from a sacrifice in time
out of love sown,
we find our way
on a path atoned;

To follow he into being resurrected
of a life redeemed,
where Christ's love be divine;
we find ourselves in the place
where immortality resides;
to have all tears wiped away from earthly strife;
is that we find to be justified
where true compassion lies.

Francis Schroeder

Beyond Horison's

Be that soul's apart
may forever bring a love shared,
never ending by time;
transcendent beyond death;
to a life eternal will we care;

While relentless, the unforgiving brings despair,
with autumn's discontent, exhales its rage,
lost are the dreams, given way to nightmares
we seek in God, the wisdom of his sage;

Poison comes with the isms, that ideology brings;
that to be saved, is enough by grace,
for faith to have wings
to fly free from this world,
of its golden cage';

Dreams are of gifts for those,
who awake to the world
visions never before heard of, nor seen,

For without dreams,
the sun will not rise to our beliefs,
where something inside us dies,
that seems never to awaken, from a deep sleep;

Paradise is in its own beauty, for the heart to realize,
only as far the imagination is willing to go,
to that of what one would dare surmise;

We choose to take our own destiny,
beyond horizons where we wish to be,
and for that,
God set the will
to be free,

Francis Schroeder

This Earthly Plain

Restless, escapes the spirit,
upon destined wind,
gentle, the morning calm with it,
stills the heart within;

To be where hope can,
that of purpose God gave,
from birth, since life began
will not wash away
on morning tide,
with castles made of sand;

There is a solace of peace to hold,
in that stare, of heart and mind,
to be found deep within the soul,
to spend in the silence of time,

What will the soul gain in the end;
when possessing that of the world,
becomes an illusion then

The substance of hope
is born eternal, of what is unseen toward the divine;
what man does or creates
becomes his own illusion, by what passes in time;

Today was yesterday's tomorrow,
and tomorrow suspends time of its sorrows;

For there are no boundaries
to mark the seasons,
of when they come or go;
but yet,
defined to us are their presence known,
by changes that take place
as they unfold'

Born the seedling of a tree sown,
to live through seasons of diversity
and out of adversity,
becomes grown

Only returning to its place of origin,
the earth called home;
eternal is the spirit for a home, also,
to the Creator known;

Responsible in this life is ours to know,
by the seeds we plant, are accountable for,
to the seasons of apropos,
for harvest fruits that faith denotes;

Do you believe,
in just what you hear, feel, and see,
or is life,
like the air you breathe

Where lies superficially,
in what you pursue so worldly
to seek what you call reality,
becomes aware of a conscience unseen,
that you take into heart of being.
Treasures you do not see,
where life is meant to be,
belonging to eternity,

It is what the spirit always knew,
walking like shadows on a landscape pursued;
born into this world
and not of it,
we are just passing through.

Francis Schroeder

In the Time of Ages

Time flows with ancestral rivers to know,
the story in your eyes to be told,
there is something to be said,
by what is moved in the rustle of a breeze blown;

To gaze upon a prairie of life's episode,
the seasons that have gone by,
from all the years of experience to rely;
generations still grow old;

Though the rain must fall;
they hear,
but do not listen;
they look,
but do not see;
as if the alien that walks among us,
walks inconspicuously;

Time crawls,
when hurt from what comes to be;
where exist from love's shadow's
comes God's wisdom,
that makes quick of time
in the passing of seasons, soon will fall,
as do
the autumn leaves;

From the vision of a dream,
launches a thousand thoughts to an imagination,
that brings the color of life,
back into a world
of black and white,
as is to reality;

For the value of wealth,
can only be measured.
by what reveals in heart,
all that can be kept for an eternity;

From where one stands,
by which befalls,
to there a place is called home for me.

Francis Schroeder

A Walk upon Event Horizons

May not know
what to do in life, but,
do know, which way how to live life,
no matter how hard,
nor how trite;

It is hard to avoid the truth,
when it is staring you in the face,
that sometimes
becomes recondite;

Nowhere to run,
nowhere to hide,
it will put you in your place,
if you do not take its side;

A place
where the eye does not see,
there is no compromise;

Equal at birth
as we may be born,
in mind and soul conformed;
when fertile is the ground for seeds sown,
it is what we do in life
with what we are born with, drawn,
that will bring growth to the exceptions
of who we are, known,
in the wake of destiny waiting to be owned,
from patience in time, grown;

Destiny
is in the tale for which we write,
in a desperate land
to see past the night;

And when doubt questions certainty at its source,
you must see beyond
what you are looking at,
to find what you are looking for;

After exploring horizons, for all there is to find,
with all things, having their place in heart and mind
returning home, to rediscover in our time,
that existing within ourselves, we left behind.

Francis Schroeder

Windows

Out past the borders of sight,
where sea and sky
seem to meet,
at an endless compromise;

Over the horizon,
where life
finds its curiosities,
that we can only come to surmise;

Staring into the distance
of space and time,
out of nonexistence
come thoughts of a mind,
that gives birth to the word,
where created are foundations,
upon which,
entire worlds are born to rise;

There by pursuit of wisdom,
that the mysteries in life
inspire imagination,
to keep within us,
our dreams alive;

And to our resolve,
we may find,
that truth is something
to be found at rest within ourselves,
whenever we seek to be wise.

Francis Schweder

For Tomorrow Never Comes

Life uncertain, in the way it goes,
what purpose will it serve
for me, does it hold,
may that I know

Where will you be,
when what is here today,
is gone tomorrow
and who you are
become unknown;
life on earth is only borrowed.
Where will you be tomorrow?

Much like the wind driven snow,
for being out in the cold,
to worry, can only be foretold,
as much as where the wind blows;

Living faith, by what it means,
is going into a future coming, you cannot see,
when riddled are tomorrow's uncertainties;
then let not waiver from the Lord, your trust,
the focus that discipline brings in loyalty;

Over there
where the lights glow,
sight be guided,
by where faith takes me to go;

That Christ died for our sins, in a sacrifice paid,
defeated death for believers, on the third day;
from yesterday
to today
and forevermore, day by day;

For never there comes tomorrow,
precarious the future that weighs,
when in the here and now.
that becomes today;
in time ordained,
by the relevance made,
for tomorrow never comes, in its wake.

Francis Schweder

Inherit the Earth

The questions of innocence
that children do ask you,
are often lost in answers,
by the time of adults, that once knew;

No closer to truth can one be, in being,
then to be the farthest,
by journey's end fleeting,
of disquiet conscience put to rest;

Do I know where my road is going;
how can my love for Jesus be enough knowing;
when from silence of the cross to believe,
is in his forgiving grace foregoing;

To find love beyond words;
to see past sunrises never seen before;
to witness a sunset at day's end,
that eyes have never caught;
comfort in a spirit to be back, when fading, the glow
is no more;

Righteousness
bears the fruit of justice,
when the world is unbalanced
in what becomes of us;

Of stranger journeys life has been;
in death be darkness,
lurks the shadows of man's sins;
where light be truth,
the sun will rise again;
love begets God's glory,
the honor that bestows victory to win;

Free are the meek within
in keeping heads without pretense,
heir to all that has been,
great will be their inheritance.

Francis Schroeder

Passing Through

Looking out across,
past an ocean of space in time;
the escape from an island prison once felt;

Life rules no island.
that onto oneself owned;
is compelled;

It is among each other,
in God's grace with Christ,
of which we dwell;

The joy of peace
from solitude in mind,
that only faith will foretell;

Born into this world and not of it;
just passing through,
and deal with what life has dealt,
on our way to heaven's gate; to be far away from hell.

Looking Across Infinity

Oh, starry sky at night,
To stare with wonder, from these eyes,
That sees past, beyond bounded shorelines;
Looking for, far across space and time;
Through Creator's windows, to be thine;
So to peer in search, deep inside;
Where faith and science, are for to find;
Sitting contrary, on opposite sides;
An expressed form of creation, evolved by it's signs,
As love from one, by intelligent design;
The answers of heart and mind;
Existentially free, in a balanced spectrum to living life;
From same origin of belief, in the Divine.

Francis Schroeder

The Hope We May Find

Beyond the horizons
in time,
is where the spirit sees past
the paradox of mind;

what profits a man that been sold
to gain the world,
only to lose his soul,
in dark of heart, is the life by a death so cold;

Through trials of tribulations
given in life,
is the perseverance of growth in patience,
that defines character out of plight;

And when life seems a lost cause
before the eyes,
then is the time to still walk by faith
and not just by sight;

Out of the sacrifices;
beneath the pain,
the hurt and sorrows,
we may come to find
out of all the thoughts that come alive
to forgive, is to put it behind;

For a new world in life shall arise,
while the old one has died;
a new purpose to find,
from a free will within, to a free man outside;

In finding hope at journey's end,
within our moral compass;
it is the soul of heart and mind,
that is deep down inside
to knowing true, in God divine,
who we are all about,
from a conscience within
that resides.

Francis Schroeder

A Walk by Faith

In flesh,
there dwelt of no good things;
of devil's advocate,
influence is evil being;
but true that come from Christ believers,
is a light to the world
for all to be seen;

Gratification
be before the divine evermore,
that our behavior
becomes the predication of scriptural law,
when we live righteous
in faith through humility,
to be that of our Lord;

It is
when you stand up
for what is morally right in faith
to win,
that gives righteousness its victory
over sin;
becomes the fire from within;

Suffering begets the character of our being,
to become better for us in knowing,
that we may be of joy to feel atoned,
while it has always been
a love unconditional sown;

Harder than truth, be the stranger
for you to know,
is accepting it;
as is truly known;

For
faith is the substance of all things hoped for,
waiting patiently to be,
the certainty in what is unseen

Francis Schroeder

The Way Back Home

Lonely is the sacrifice,
freedom from the sins in our strife,
the redemption of a free will
given in life;

With humbling does not pontificate
from what discourse that remains,
riding upon winds of change
in manifest honor prevailing,
against those who wrong,
that rein;
that whatever tomorrow may bring this way.
Divine be God's glory,
never again, shall we be afraid,

To breathe deep
for inspiration to come alive;
in every word you say;
by the way you live in kind
and in every word you write;
just as,
in every breath you take
that gives you life;

As it is not so much
of where you have been
from what was known;

As it is,
how well you deal with
to where you are going;

And when all roads delude to Rome;
patience
is the wisdom taken to be told,
by way in faith to follow;

For be careful
the journeys on which you roam,
hardest is the road
back to home;
that only one
stands out alone,
where truth found
is known,
the way that will lead you home;

Francis Schroeder

To One's Own

Bitterness; to each, that which, belongs our own,
in the heart does know,
its joy others cannot share,
from where one goes;

There is a comfort
in the quiet of solitude at rest,
the absence of sound by words borrowed,
to play upon a soul's caress;

Happiness for the moment, is only contemporary;
to know true in oneself of belief
that grace be divine, real is the rhythm of joy,
the truth is sight for to see,
from sinful world, to be set free;

Finding true, that measure of peace inside,
when yesterday's tomorrow
has always been here today,
where life's darkest hour fades away, in time;

In perseverance,
is for hope to never end;
with God,
all things are possible,
in faith that can;

In the presence of angels so fine,
within radiance of a soul in Christ;
love is the heart in trust
that cares enough,
for the willingness of self-sacrifice;
unconditional in life,
makes it worth the price;

No matter the obligation or servitude,
in search of character, for who you are to be;
never forget,
your soul is always your own
forever to keep;
naked in its responsibility; held accountable
for God to see;
so that throughout the vastness echoes of life,
for all eternity.

Francis Schroeder

By a Measure of Grace

Answers that whisper
upon a silent breeze
an ancient voice familiar to me,
an old friend that I know
to place across time,
to be free as the wind blows;

To see again as a child,
the beauty of a rose
before the eyes beholden
the windows of the soul;

Complacent that may be in heart
becomes that protected innocence known
you once knew from afar, that was your own,
yet you asked; where did the time go?
for what changes
the seasons will bring,
are in the heart
that songs will sing;

There is no measure in time,
nor by success to be traced,
that defines life to the value
of which it is to be placed;

But from the love
that grows in heart,
that holds true
in every day we must face;

By what is found from seeds we plant,
in the absence of impatient hast,
that are compassionate
by God's grace;

Speak with all conviction,
we live in the grace
by which we are saved.

The Truth in a Name

To begin is fifty percent
into a journey of a thousand miles,
with the first step;

Saved by grace
through faith in Christ
is a covenant kept

What we do with life from then on,
is the other fifty percent,
held accountable by which we are met;
day by day

For who we are,
to know where we are going,
is destination reached, for our own sake;
standing before the edge,
walking upon the dawn of events horizon,
determines that
by which befalls us to our fate;

To reject truth,
is denying the source of origin
from where we came;
the illusions fed to the hungry,
still make them
for who they are today;

It will be by fruits of labors availed,
that you will know them,
in portrayal;
the discipline of heart,
that gives that value,
the virtues of mind
found by the light of day;

Where truth is the power within faith,
and not by sight,
found in Jesus Christ as the life,
of whom to earth he came;
in the righteousness that speaks his name,
reveals true of who we are
by the heart of many thoughts
reflected in our ways,

Destiny's Honor

It is in the presence of angels to find,
there is a power of soul;
life as we now know,
is but a passing dream in mind;

Deep within the search for worlds,
beyond the signature of hidden skies,
we ride on majestic waves,
legend in our own space and time;

Traveling on roads
of unknown signs
that are already set,
with attitudes open to foresight;

We cast our sails
into the known winds of faith,
to trust thine will,
take us to our fate,

Should the sun rise
before our eyes, another day,
it is by the good will,
for an unfinished life
of the given way,
from one so gracious and great;

That God is not done with the rough path
of our written ways;

To take the road less traveled
for life to be brave,
that one day you must face;

To honor with regard, that puts others before yourself,
without regret nor complaint;
let compassion be its grace;

We are our own expression,
to say of whom
we represent,
from where we came;

And every time a long journey comes at its end to lay,
we return back somewhere
to be called home again;

In another place,
somewhere in time,
there is always hope to relate;
looking beyond the horizon
to be true in our hearts, with Christ,
is in honor of our destiny,
to be at heaven's gate.

Francis Schroeder

The Epilogue

The strife
for eternal life,
belongs to another scope defined,
that has always been part of us within,
leaving behind the dimension of sin,
with no end to find,
nowhere to begin,
beyond creation,
of all its evolutionary signs;

That only in Christ
is the life to know,
where found: becomes home.

Being justified by faith,
We have peace with God
Through our Lord Jesus Christ.

Romans Ch. 5 v. 1
King James version

From the author,

Life has never been a bowl full of cherries. Passionate the thought may be: still remains foolish at best… Beware the illusions with a dream, pursued by dreamers deceived, deprives prosperity in test of time, chasing winds they will never find.

> "If you tell a lie big enough and keep repeating it, people will eventually come to believe it. The lie can be maintained only for such time as the State can shield the people from political, economic, and/or military consequence of the lie. It thus becomes vitally important for the State to use all of its powers to repress dissent, for the truth is the mortal enemy of the lie, and thus by extension, the truth is the greatest enemy of the State."
> —Joseph Goebbels

> "By their fruit you will recognize them."
> —Matthew 7:16

> "A lie gets halfway around the world before the truth has a chance to get its pants on."
> —Winston Churchill

> "If you hold to my teaching, you are really my disciples. Then you will know the truth, and the truth will set you free."
> —John 8:31-32

A mirror given, reflecting those who live in glass houses from where they cast stones. The greatest lie ever told on earth, is that the Devil does not exist, who deceives us from God. Without God, without Jesus Christ we lose our identity of who we are in moral conscience to lies, blinding us from righteous discernment.

"I am the way and the truth and the life. No one comes to the Father except through me."
—John 14:6

Villainous be the school master we do not know, in a reality unfamiliar: "Behold, I send you forth as sheep in the midst of wolves; be ye therefore wise as serpents, and harmless as doves." Matthew 10:16 Through faith, God will deliver us out of adversity that shows purpose and gives meaning for what we seek. Whereas, I leave you with the challenge this book might offer is to think from where we came, to where we are going; from where we stand at present relevant in soul and truth.

CPSIA information can be obtained
at www.ICGtesting.com
Printed in the USA
BVHW071601170220
572579BV00007B/936